50 Crazy Romantic Things to do in Iceland

Text copyright © Snæfríður Ingadóttir 2009
Photographs copyright © Þorvaldur Örn Kristmundsson 2009
Translation: Kristín Birgisdóttir and Darren Foreman

Copyright © 2009 - SALKA PUBLISHER - REYKJAVÍK
www.salka.is

ISBN 978-9979-650-75-1

Design and layout: Arnar Geir Ómarsson 2009

Printed in Oddi, Iceland

Thanks to:
Matthías Kristjánsson, Ragnar Axelsson, Sigurður Jökull, Héðinn Ólafsson,
Guðrún Stella Gissurardóttir, Helga Ingadóttir, IPA/Corbis.

50
CRAZY
ROMANTIC
things to do
in Iceland

Snæfríður Ingadóttir
Þorvaldur Örn Kristmundsson

Salka

1.
Lay down

Iceland is one of the few countries on the planet that is free of mosquitoes and ants. In fact, due to the country's isolation and the relatively recent effects of the last ice age, it has very few insects at all compared to the rest of Europe. So use the opportunity to lie down as often as possible, either in the next clearing or in a nice hollow, and make out with your loved one. It's even a nice idea to sleep outside for one night. When you've found a nice spot, join two sleeping bags together and keep each other warm and cozy until you wake up with the first sunbeam and singing birds.

2.
Hook a meal

Ice fishing is an invigorating sport, but one that requires a lot of patience. So what better way to pass the time on the frozen ice than snuggling up under a big blanket with the one you fancy? Along with the obvious items (hook, line, bait, something to cut a hole in the ice, and warm clothing) bring a hearty lunch and warm beverage and head out to one of the many popular lakes in the Reykjavík area: Elliðavatn, Hafravatn, Urriðavatn and Reynisvatn. It must be said that it gives one a tickling feeling to move the line up and down in the water: it makes the mind look forward to a romantic night where the catch is made into a lovely meal and the hunter will get his reward.

3.
Swim with seals

Seals are unbelievably charming and interesting animals that are said to have human eyes. It's fun to watch these creatures from a distance but way more interesting to see them up close; so if you dare, you and your loved one should jump into the ice cold sea and share the unique experience of swimming among them. There are mainly two types of seals that live around Iceland: the harbour seal and the grey seal. These curious animals often come very close to swimmers and it's beautiful to see how smoothly they glide through the water. Just be careful, for although these creatures are charming, they can also be dangerous if threatened. For information about seals and seal-watching contact The Icelandic Seal Centre in Hvammstangi **(www.selasetur.is)**.

MY OWN ROMANTIC THINGS

_____

_____

_____

_____

_____

_____

50.
Enjoy the midnight sun

Over the summer time you can barely notice the difference between day and night. Icelandic summer nights are not only bright, but also tranquil, magical and long. It doesn't matter where you are on the island, it's simply a wonderful experience to see the sun go almost down, tiptoe on the horizon, and then suddenly rise up again. Taking a walk on a bright, sunny night is a memorable thing and allows for all sorts of activities ...

Play 49. in the snow

In Iceland it doesn't matter what time of year it is, you can always find a place to practice winter sports, as 10% of the country is constantly covered with snow. You can choose between nine glaciers along with other smaller areas which are always covered with the white stuff. Get your ski gear on and let a big jeep take you up to the top. Zoom around on a snowmobile, play snow golf, or slide down the steep hills on a big plastic bag. It's perfect to end the day in a warm bed, where you can melt a glacial ice cube on your partner's body, lick it off, and ... mmm!

48.
Take a walk on the wild side

The majority of Iceland's 103.000 square kilometres is wilderness where you can find beautiful mountains, big rivers, pitch-black lava, hot wells, magnificent canyons and snow-white glaciers. The wilderness is also home to elves, trolls and wild animals, and the silence is as overwhelming as the fresh, clean air. Over the summer time it's really romantic to get adventurous and go camping with your loved one far away from everything. You can, for instance, go to the biggest national park in Europe, Vatnajökull National Park, and take challenging hikes. The possibilities are endless. Just remember to let others know where you're going and check on the weather report because, although the Icelandic wilderness is fascinating, you can also run into all kinds of danger, such as eruptions, earthquakes, storms, avalanches, and river floods.

Share 47. an easter egg

Icelanders are famous for eating enormous amounts of chocolate eggs over Easter. They are produced by the million right before the holiday and come in all kinds of sizes and types. Most are filled with various kinds of candy, such as caramels, licorice, jelly, and chocolate covered raisins. They also contain a fortune: wise words which may affect your life. For example: "Many people change into monkeys around money; The wiser one relents; and Few things are so good that they can't get better." You can even buy special love eggs, which are extra big and made for couples to share. You should, of course, eat as much as you possibly can, since research has confirmed that chocolate increases the libido.

46.
Let runes reveal the answers

If you and your partner want to get a peek into the future, Iceland is the right place to do so. Icelanders' belief in the unknown is very strong and they frequently visit fortune-tellers and psychics to look for answers. Let these people give you a glimpse into your future by using runes, which are ancient letters from the Vikings. Are you really meant for each other? How many children will you have? Are some difficulties ahead and how can you conquer them? These ancient runes are very reliable and can also be used as your very own protection symbol.

45. Enjoy an outdoor massage

The Blue Lagoon **(www.bluelagoon.is)**, is one of the most popular tourist attractions in Iceland. There you can experience a heavenly and memorable head to toe massage while floating around the Lagoon on an inflatable mattress and looking up at the blue sky. What could be more relaxing or romantic? And once you're in the mood, why not go all the way, as the Blue Lagoon is also a popular place to tie the knot. Forget the fancy clothes and decorated hall; say your "I do's" in your swim suits with the hot and steamy wonders of nature all around.

44. Celebrate love

In general, Icelanders are very liberal when it comes to lifestyle and sex, which is most clearly evidenced by the Gay Pride celebration **(www.gaypride.is)**, held yearly since 1999 and is now the city's biggest festival. From Thursday to Sunday during the second week in August, the entire city seems to ooze with a truly gay feeling, in both the old and new meanings of the word. The festival reaches its peak at the Gay Pride Parade, with more than 50,000 gay and straight revellers gathering to celebrate love and life in a dancing, singing, hot carnival vibe!

43.
Strenghten your look as a couple

To emphasize the seriousness of your relationship it's of course necessary to wear the same outfit when you're out in public. If you want to take it further than a matching jogging set bargained for at a "two-for-one" store you should check out the Icelandic brands Cintamani and 66° North **(www.cintamani.is and www.66north.com)**. They make popular and trendy outdoor clothing for both genders. Leave no one in doubt that you're a couple and still walk proudly hand in hand down Laugavegur, Reykjavík's main shopping street, where people from all over town go to look at others and show themselves off.

42. Sleep in a turf hut

From the first settlement until the mid-20th century the majority of Icelanders lived in turf huts. While other nations built houses from timber and concrete, Icelanders used soil and grass, constructing snug spaces with low ceilings. Family members and guests usually shared the same bedroom, not only because of a lack of space, but also to keep each other warm. One can imagine the action that resulted from such a situation! There are still plenty of turf huts all over Iceland and many of them are used as museums. In Sænautasel at Jökuldalsheiði it's even possible to stay in one. With no electricity, water, or wc, it's certainly no four-star hotel. But snuggling together under a warm blanket, with the natural and primitive smell of the turf all around you, takes you back in time and keeps you close (literally) to nature.

41.
Enjoy the music of nature

In the northern part of the country you can attend an extraordinary outdoor concert all year round! This modern masterpiece emanates from the most powerful waterfall in Europe, called Dettifoss, in the Jökulsá River. The 44 m high, 100 m wide falls makes a stunning soundtrack as you picnic on a blanket next to the river, with sounds no orchestra could ever imitate. And this concert is not only free – it's endless! Instead of applauding the unforgettable event, you might find other ways of showing your appreciation ...

40.
Wake up in a rustic romance

Although Iceland is known for its rough nature, it's possible to have a softer experience at one of the country's many romantic countryside hotels. Two of these cozy getaways, Hotel Búðir **(www.budir.is)** and Hotel Rangá **(www.hotelranga.is)**, have several times been named the most romantic hotels in Iceland. Hotel Búðir is located on the Snæfellsnes peninsula. It takes two hours to get there from Reykjavík, but if you're really in a hurry the hotel has a helicopter available for pick-ups. The view from the hotel is spectacular, with Snæfellsjökull glacier rising just beyond the front door. Hotel Rangá is in the south part of the country. In addition to its secluded and romantic setting, the hotel is located next to one of the country's most generous salmon rivers.

39.
Learn Icelandic folk dances

If you've tried the classical pair dances, such as salsa, waltz, and tango, then the next step is to try the Icelandic folk dances. These ring dances were developed from old folklores, which the dancers sing along with. The rhythm and steps can vary, but they are basically similar to the well-known Faroe Islands dance, or Vikivaki. In addition to the steps, dancers also use a series of hand-holds and lifts, always moving clockwise. The dances are not only original and fun, but seem to bring the partners closer together, as the marriage of meaning and movement gets the blood flowing and warms the heart.

38.
Linger on love week

Every August the town of Bolungarvík in the West Fjords organizes a Love Week, during which everyone is welcome to participate in a celebration of love. All week long the locals light red candles, decorate their homes with hearts, and send their loved ones special love-week cards. All kinds of courses are also offered, for instance in how to kiss and hug or give a sensual massage. Corny love songs are played in every house, store, and bar, and the locals try to be super affectionate the entire week. Love Week will leave you with lots of romantic and sexy memories. And as many an attendee can attest, you might receive a surprising little gift nine months later.

37.
Be cabin guards

In the wilderness of Iceland there are a number of cabins, built by volunteers from the travel organizations, in which travelers on their way over the highlands may spend a night. If you really want to be far away from all distractions, enjoying the wilderness and solitude, you can apply to be a cabin guard. It's a perfect job for couples, and since travelers often don't show up for days at a time, there's a very good chance you'll have the place all to yourselves. The pay varies and sometimes there's no pay at all; but it's truly irrelevant when given the opportunity of living in your own cabin with the unspoiled nature all around.

36.
Celebrate
the winter

The Winter Lights Festival is an annual event held every February in Reykjavík, designed to stimulate and enliven city life and celebrate both the winter and the growing light after a long period of darkness. The program is a mixture of art and industry, environment and history, sports and culture; and the events provide entertainment for both visitors and locals alike. The entire city is beautifully lit during the festival, creating a perfect environment for people in love. Dress warmly, since most of the program is outside, and then enjoy the festival as you get to know the interesting and varied faces of Iceland.

35.
Rent a summer cottage

When Icelanders want to relax they leave town to seek the tranquility of the countryside, often staying in summer houses. These cozy little villas can be rented, but in recent years it has become more popular to own one. It's not uncommon to find the more scenic areas of the country dotted with the little cottages, with the south being the most popular spot. These romantic hideaways come in all shapes and sizes and typically feature a hot tub and a gas grill. So sign up for a weekend away from it all, and be inventive: take some champagne and romantic music with you ... and don't forget the massage oil. After a long day's activities, indoors or out, it could come in handy.

34.
Get
Snowed
in

The Icelandic weather can get very bad at times. When it snows, roads and schools are often closed, the electricity goes off, and people get trapped inside their houses until they can dig themselves out. Iceland is also one of the windiest areas in the world and in several places the gusts regularly reach speeds of up to 30 meters/second (67 mph), the first level of a hurricane. So when the weather is showing its worst side, it´s nice to stay inside and watch the craziness through the window. But it can also be exciting to go out and face the weather. If you choose the second option, just hold each other tight, so you don't blow away. And please don't go so far that the rescue squad has to look for you … the adventure could become a little too costly.

33.
Indulge yourself

Due to the hot water which pours out of the Icelandic ground, outdoor pools and hot tubs can be found all over the island and are open from morning to night all year round. Natives visit them regularly, as they know how soothing the water is for body and soul and what a sensational feeling it is to sit in a hot tub (38 – 44°C) sensing the water all over you. For those of you who want even more pampering, you can spend an entire day in the five-star Laugar spa in Reykjavík **(www.laugarspa.is)**, connected to the country's biggest pool, Laugardalslaug. Guests of the spa can choose between a variety of amenities, including saunas, steam rooms, hot tubs, and even a restaurant. For a completely relaxing experience, couples can book a massage together, enjoy a light dinner while still in their robes, and finish by dozing together in a comfy recliner in front of the fireplace.

32. Follow the path of the outlaws

The most famous love story in Iceland concerns the 18th century outlaws Fjalla-Eyvindur and Halla – the Bonnie and Clyde of Iceland. With Fjalla-Eyvindur wanted for a crime he didn't commit, the pair spent 40 years hiding out in the ice-cold mountains, forced to steal horses and sheep for survival. They became experts at living off the harsh and unforgiving land and were, for example, the first Icelanders to boil food in a geothermal well. Neither darkness, cold, hunger, nor the long arm of the law could destroy their love, and though they were arrested several times they always managed to escape and make it back to one another. In Hveravellir and Hvannalindir it's still possible to see the ruins of cabins where they hid out. The story of Fjalla-Eyvindur and Halla is well worth getting to know, as it definitely teaches you that love can conquer all.

31.
Take your love to the edge

Fetch your binoculars, blanket and a bird manual and take a walk to the coast, where you can crawl to the edge of a cliff and watch birds roosting or in flight. Around 300 species have been observed in Iceland, with the biggest colony, containing millions of seabirds, located in Látrabjarg in the West Fjords. The most common bird on the island is the puffin, a very cute bird with a nose like a clown and the look of a pastor. The biggest puffin colony in the world is in Vestmannaeyjar (The Westmen Isles). Other common species at the shore are the auk, black guillemot, fulmar and gannet. For those who think bird watching is only for nerds and in no way romantic, try the following game: name all the birds you see and the one who gets the higher score wins. Include sex favors in the prize and the competition will get even more exciting.

30.
Drive around Iceland in 24 hours

Over the summer time in Iceland it literally doesn't get dark. Bright summer nights offer many opportunities, so save the sleeping for winter and get busy. One especially fun and challenging idea is to drive around the island in 24 hours, taking in every bit of the wonderful scenery! The road around Iceland (Road nr. 1) is 1339 km long and encircles most of the island (excluding the West Fjords and inner highlands). Take along some food and music and hit the road! A road trip like this is also perfect for you to talk about your dreams and future together.

29.
Play the gift game

Kolaportið is the biggest flea market in Iceland, located indoors at the Reykjavík harbor. The market is only open on weekends and is very colorful, offering everything, new and used: food, books, clothing, jewelry, cd's and much more. It's fun to walk around the market with your partner, but even more fun to play the gift game, where you look for unique little gifts for each other. The rules are simple: decide how long you're going to shop and how much you're going to spend and set off exploring. Then, at a designated time, meet up at the flea market's coffee house and exchange gifts. The joy of giving and the surprise of receiving might lead to very interesting results.

Do like 28.
John and
Yoko

Over the peak of wintertime (Nov. - Jan.) the sun barely shows itself in Iceland and the days are almost as dark as nights. Many find it difficult to wake up during this time and there are very few things more cozy than staying under a warm cover when darkness and cold rule outdoors. So why not indulge yourself and spend several days in bed with the one you love? In 1969 John Lennon and Yoko Ono spent 8 days in bed at a hotel in Montréal, Canada and were not bored for one minute! So give it a try. Explore each other, trade massages, discuss your plans and dreams, or watch a string of your favorite movies. You could even write a song while you're at it, as Lennon did with *Give Peace a Chance*.

27.
Get sweaty together

Every year thousands of people participate in the Reykjavík Marathon **(www.marathon.is)**, which is held the weekend closest to Reykjavík's anniversary on the 18th of August. You don't need much running experience to participate, as there are routes of varying lengths (3, 10, 21 and 42 km), with runners of all ages and abilities participating. Children are even invited to do a 1 km run. Lots of foreign runners come to sweat alongside Icelanders and participate in the "Menningarnótt" (Culture Night) feast later that day. After having burned some calories together it's a must to visit one of the many coffee houses in Reykjavík, and eat as much as you can of cakes and gourmet fare, which you certainly deserve after the run. Later you can get to know Icelandic music, art and acting during the Culture Night, as well as reveling in the carnival atmosphere that engulfs the city.

26.
Take the plunge between continents

Þingvellir is a national park about 50 km from Reykjavík which contains a spectacular rift called Silfra, definitely the most beautiful diving spot in the country and also on most of the world's lists of top-ten diving spots. The crystal-clear glacial water neither freezes nor rises above 4 degrees, which contributes to the amazing visibility of up to 150 meters. But the rift, which is a real treasure, also has another claim to fame: as it lies between the Eurasian and American plates, you can actually dive between two continents ... without a visa! It is unbelievably romantic to swim around in this picturesque area, looking into caves and using body language to communicate. If you don't have a dive license, don't worry, you can still snorkel in the rift and enjoy the scenery.

25.
Fly on the wings of love

Do you remember when you first met and your hearts beat faster every time you looked at each other and you were literally high on love? In Iceland you can reawaken that tickling feeling by taking a private flight over the island. Although it's a great feeling to float among the clouds with your loved one, don't forget to look down. Icelandic nature is striking from above: sometimes like a painting, with complex colors and patterns, moss-covered lava, glaciers, mountains and hot, colorful wells. If all this is not enough to get your heart beating faster, then ask your pilot to take a dive – that should do it for you!

24. Hop on a horse

Horseback riding in the Icelandic countryside with the person you love is a wonderful experience. And if it's your first time you don't have to fear because Icelandic horses are small, stable, strong and good tempered, making them perfect for beginners on a romantic tour. The Icelandic horse can go fast if you want to and is the only horse in the world that utilizes five gaits: Walk, trot, canter, gallop and tölt, which is a sort of smooth trot. Since the 11th century it has been forbidden to import horses to Iceland, which is why the Icelandic horse has developed without any influence from other breeds. For that reason it has been able to keep several qualities that other European breeds have lost, especially regarding gaits and colors.

23.
Go back to childhood

Some wise person said that we don't stop playing because we grow old, we grow old because we stop playing. In Iceland it's easy to keep your inner child alive with memories of sandboxes and sandcastles, as the island has more black sand beaches than anywhere in the world. They surround almost the entire island and are actually made of volcanic ash. Take your loved one for a walk on a black beach and tell each other memories from childhood and you will definitely get to know each other better. Although black beaches are in the majority in Iceland, there are also a few white ones, the most beautiful one located at Skarðsvík, Snæfellsnes.

22.Get deep together

As a result of Iceland's thousands of volcanic eruptions and earthquakes, many underground caves have been formed. In the old days Icelanders used them as shelter for their sheep and even to live in, but they are also perfect for romantic and mystical excursions under the earth. One of the deepest lava caves in the world is Þríhnjúkahellir (nearly 200 meters), located only a few kilometers from Reykjavík northwest of Bláfjöll. What could be more exhilarating to the senses than venturing into that dark unknown with someone you want to be close to, especially since there's no place as perfect for candles and romance as a deep and secluded cave! All you need is good equipment, headlamps, climbing experience – and courage.

21.
Feed the ducks

Here is some advice for couples who are hesitating to start a family. Buy some bread or biscuits and go down to The Pond in the centre of Reykjavík early on a Saturday or Sunday morning. There you will see families gathered at the water's edge feeding the ducks, geese and swans. There's often a lot of action, with laughing children, proud parents, and happy (and completely stuffed) birds. This romantic picture of parenthood and family life might just convince you to take that next step.

20.
Celebrate the summer solstice

The night before the 24th of June, or Jónsmessa (Midsummer's Day), is said to be one of the most magical of the year, according to Icelandic myths. All over the country Icelanders celebrate, making campfires, taking long walks in the night, or dancing and singing out in the nature. You might even see them rolling naked in the grass, which is said to bring good fortune and health. The outdoor organization, Útivist **(www.utivist.is)**, has for many years organized a special Jónsmessa-walk from Skógar to Þórsmörk. Winding through some of the country's most beautiful and romantic scenery, the walk has been very popular with both couples and those traveling alone, with hundreds of people participating yearly.

19.
Bathe under blue sky

In Iceland you can find lots of natural hot springs and pools, with temperatures from 24-48 Celsius. There's nothing more relaxing than lying in the warm water and enjoying the wide and rustic panorama. The most common natural pools are located in Landmannalaugar and in Hveravellir, but asking the locals could be a clever move, as they might share some secret spots with you. For example, in the south part of the country it's possible to bathe in the hot spring Heiti Lækur in Hveragerði. It takes one to two hours to walk there from Hveragerði and the reward for the trek is a nice hot bath in a long and crooked spring where it's really easy to find a hidden place just for the two of you.

18.
Swing in
Vestmannaeyjar

There is one activity which is a must-do for everyone who visits Vestmannaeyjar (The Westmen Isles). "Spranga" is a sport which was first practiced by mountain climbers who wanted to retrieve the eggs of nesting seabirds and consists mostly of pushing oneself away from the steep cliffs and swinging in wide arcs above the ocean below. Experienced swingers even manage giant spins and somersaults. No trip to Vestmannaeyjar is complete without at least giving the sport a try, as there's no better way to pump up your adrenalin and prove your courage to your better half.

17.
Make out at the movies

Movie houses have always been good places for dates, which may be why Icelanders are such enthusiastic moviegoers. In fact, Iceland boasts a higher movie attendance than most other countries and even makes more movies, per capita, than Hollywood! But Icelandic movie houses differ from others in one obvious way: at its halfway point, the movie will stop and the lights will come up for a ten-minute break. Guests can then stretch their legs, share their opinions about the film, get a snack refill, or simply make out with their partners.

16.
Cool down

How would you like to offer your loved one an ice-cold, refresh-ing cocktail made from the biggest glacier in Europe? Pack up your favorite spirits, an ice pick and cocktail shaker, and head for the Jökulsárlón lagoon, in the east part of the country. The lagoon is a dazzling display of floating icebergs in an endless range of blue from the Vatnajökull Glacier. Take the boat trip through these floating sculptures and you can toast with a drink made from 1500 year old ice, with the unforgettable scen-ery as backdrop. But if you don't have time to go that far, you can always visit the Ice Bar, in Stokkseyri **(www.icelandic-wonders.is)** or Restaurant Reykjavík **(www.restaurant-reykjavik.is)** These hot spots serve cool cocktails in rooms chilled to below zero ... which means that any heat you want is going to have to come from you and your partner.

15. Hit the beach

The ingenuity of Icelanders has no limits. With so much hot water bubbling out of the ground, some genius got the idea to funnel some out into the sea, warming the ocean and allowing for the creation of a beach right in the middle of Reykjavík. Known as the Ylströndin, or Warm Beach, this white sand oasis was opened in Nauthólsvík in 2000 and has been extremely popular with city residents, who race to the area at the first sign of sun. Used as both a bathing and picnic area, the beach has all the modern facilities: rest rooms, showers, snack bar, a little pool for those who still find the ocean too cold, and even volleyball and sailing.

14.
Steal a kiss behind a waterfall

Off Road nr. 1 between Hvolsvöllur and Skógar you can find a spectacular waterfall called Seljalandsfoss. The 60 meter high wall of water is perfect for memorable photographs, but it also keeps a very romantic secret: it's possible to walk behind the falls without getting wet! So sweep your loved one away and steal a kiss right in the middle of the path. And who knows, go at a time when there are no other visitors and the kiss might turn into something more …

13.
Ice skate on the pond

On ice cold winter days there is nothing more romantic than ice skating on a frozen pond. When the temperature drops and the water freezes, Reykjavík residents flock to Tjörnin, the big pond in the centre of town. Although there are indoor rinks both in Reykjavík and Akureyri, it's much more fun to be outside, skating together under the stars. And afterwards it's perfect to go into the café in the City Hall, which is built right over the pond, and enjoy a hot and cozy cup of cocoa.

12.
Sail to the island of love

Flatey, in Breiðafjörður **(www.flatey.is)**, is a tiny island bathed in a timeless, romantic atmosphere. Life on the island seems from a bygone era: cars are not allowed (though travelers and their luggage can be picked up by tractor) and visitors are encouraged to put away their cell phones ... all the better to enjoy the tranquil and beautiful surroundings. Though only two families inhabit the island full-time, most of the original homes, built in the early 1900's, are still in use as summer houses. The island's little church is quite unique and the restaurant and hotel are full of charm. Whether staying on the island or just spending the day, you can't help but be affected by the quaint and romantic feeling lingering in the air.

11. Have food and fun

Every year chefs from all over the world descend on Reykjavík for the Food and Fun festival **(www.foodandfun.is)**. Combining their culinary talents with Iceland's freshest ingredients, the chefs dazzle local diners eager for a memorable night out. The smell of world-class cuisine tunes up the senses, spicing up the love life and making it a perfect time for romantic wining and dining. Guests can even watch cooking contests, which gets the mouth watering and stomach singing. And after having satisfied the taste buds, keep the enticing flavor alive by dancing late into the night at one of the city's many downtown clubs.

10. Increase your libido with rope yoga

Rope yoga **(www.ropeyoga.com)** is a powerful training system designed by Icelander Guðni Gunnarsson which strengthens mind, body and soul – not to mention the sex drive. It has been extremely popular in both Iceland and Hollywood, where the stars flock to the sessions. The exercises, which apply focus, breathing and force to strengthen the body and burn calories, are performed with special ropes fastened to the hands and feet. The exertion increases circulation to the middle part of the body and, therefore, to the genitalia, which may also increase the libido. So visit your nearest fitness centre and sign you and your lover up for a healthy ... and sexy ... rope yoga session.

9. State your vows like the vikings

If a church wedding does not fascinate you, you could get married heathen-style, like the Vikings. Icelanders were heathens until the year 1000 when Christianity was legalized, but there are still many who practice these beliefs; in fact, they are getting more numerous every year. In 1972 the Ásatrú organization **(www.asatru.is)**, was formed which builds on Icelandic/Nordic folklore and the spirits and entities the folklore represents. Heathen weddings are most often held outside and are presided over by a chieftain, or "goði". The couple states their vows aloud and then drinks from a sheep horn while holding a ring symbolizing eternity. Fire plays a big part as well. All in all the ceremony is more personal and liberal then a church wedding.

8.
Admire the dance of northern lights

There's nothing more romantic then walking with your loved one under a colorful sky of dancing northern lights (aurora borealis). They occur exclusively near the poles and can only be seen during certain conditions, mainly between September and April, usually when the sky is clear, the temperature is freezing, and the moon not too bright. The lights can appear in various colors and forms and may be either still or seen dancing around the sky. This spectacular show can easily melt every heart and if there are two of them they will definitely find each other's beat and merge into one.

Fight 7. with ghosts

At first you might not think of ghosts as romantic things. But you can be sure that if you have to stay in a haunted house it's very good to have someone you love and trust to cling to when things start to get scary. And the unique circumstances often make the relationship stronger. One of the most famous haunted houses in Iceland is the mountain cabin in Hvítarnes at Kjölur, built in 1930. Guests of the cabin have reported hearing strange sounds and seeing the image of a woman with long, dark hair. It is even said that she occasionally makes physical contact by lying down on every male who dares to sleep in a certain bed.

6.
Get your wishes granted

It is said that if you hike to the top of Helgafell (Holy Mountain) on the Snæfellsnes peninsula you can get three wishes fulfilled. So what better destination if your partner is reluctant to tie the knot? Certain steps must be followed, though, for your trip to be successful. The walk begins at the grave of Guðrún Ósvífursdóttir, who is a well-known character from The Icelandic Sagas. Climb to the top without speaking or glancing backwards until you come to the temple ruins. Now face east and make your wishes. For them to come true they must be made with a guileless heart and never revealed to anyone.

5. Make a love spell

In Iceland every third marriage ends in divorce – just as in the rest of the western world. So if you're really committed to making your marriage work for a lifetime you should cover your back with a solid and old-fashioned love spell. From the early ages people have tried to utilize the hidden powers for their benefit and Icelanders are no exception. You can also learn all about witchcraft, love spells and other spells in a very unique museum in Strandir, called Galdrasetrið **(www.stranda galdur.is)**.

4.
Practice super soft outdoor sex

In Iceland you can find countless places to practice outdoor sex without any disturbance. You don't have to go far off Road nr. 1 to find nice mating places, as most of the island is completely uninhabited. And as a bonus attraction, the earth is very often covered with ever-so-soft moss, which takes the lovemaking to an even higher level. In Iceland there are over 600 species of moss, many of them with a velvety texture that increases sensations when it touches the naked skin.